I0137298

William Buell Sprague

Glorifying God in the Fires

A Discourse Delivered in the Second Presbyterian Church, Albany,

November 28, 1861, the Day of the Annual Thanksgiving, in the State of

New York

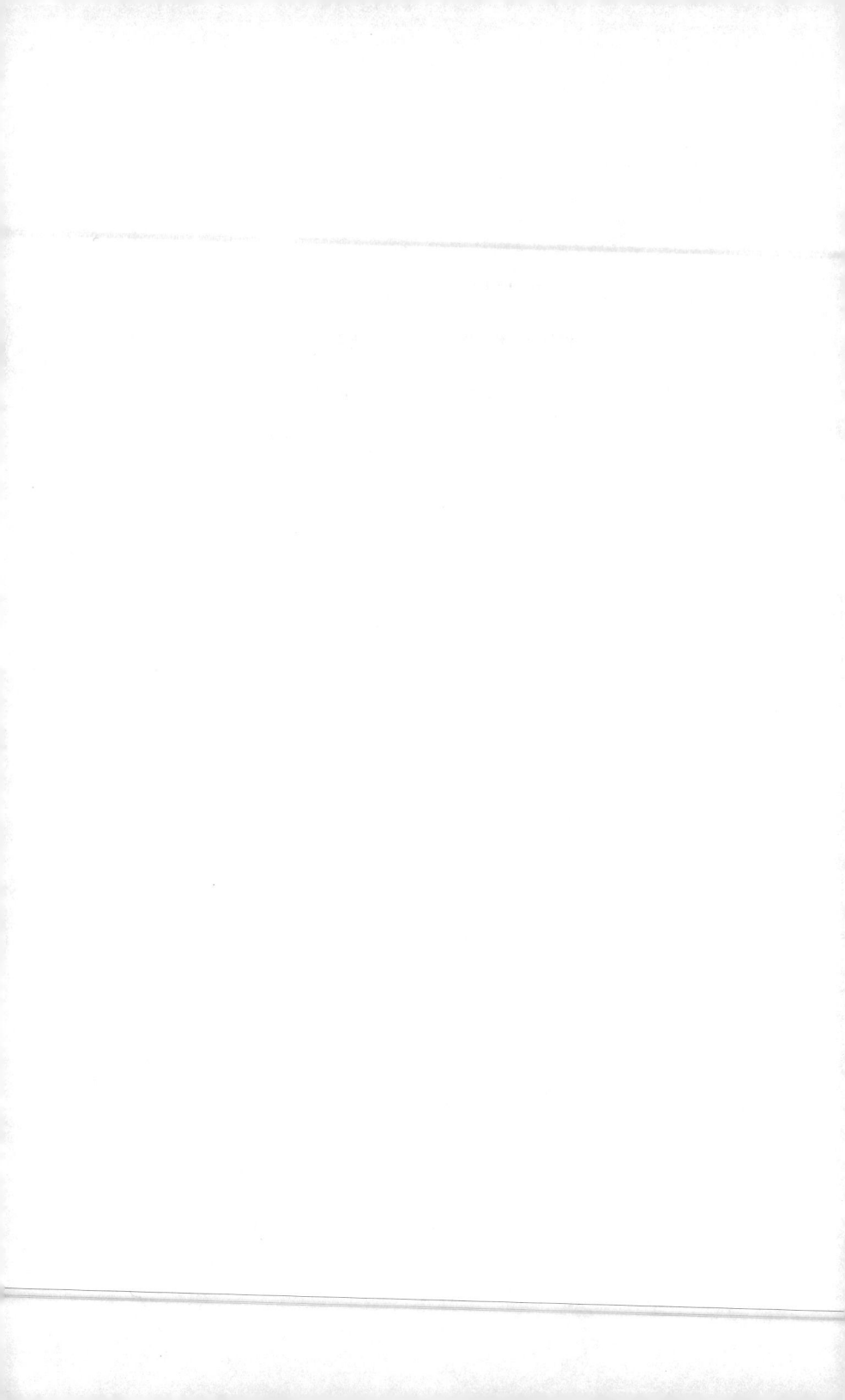

William Buell Sprague

Glorifying God in the Fires
*A Discourse Delivered in the Second Presbyterian Church, Albany, November 28,
1861, the Day of the Annual Thanksgiving, in the State of New York*

ISBN/EAN: 9783337255091

Printed in Europe, USA, Canada, Australia, Japan

Cover: Foto ©Lupo / pixelio.de

More available books at **www.hansebooks.com**

Glorifying God in the Fires.

A

DISCOURSE

DELIVERED IN THE

SECOND PRESBYTERIAN CHURCH, ALBANY,

NOVEMBER 28, 1861, THE DAY OF

THE ANNUAL THANKSGIVING,

IN THE STATE OF NEW YORK.

BY WILLIAM B. SPRAGUE, D. D.

PUBLISHED BY REQUEST OF THE YOUNG MEN OF THE CONGREGATION.

ALBANY:
PRINTED BY C. VAN BENTHUYSEN.
1861.

A few sentences have been added since the delivery.

TO

MAJOR GENERAL MᶜCLELLAN,

COMMANDER IN CHIEF

OF THE ARMY OF THE UNITED STATES,

THIS DISCOURSE

IS MOST RESPECTFULLY INSCRIBED,

WITH PROFOUND ADMIRATION

FOR THE UNSURPASSED ABILITY

AND HEROIC DEVOTION TO

THE INTERESTS OF HIS COUNTRY,

WITH WHICH HE IS CONDUCTING

THE GRANDEST MILITARY ENTERPRISE

OF THE AGE.

DISCOURSE.

ISAIAH XXIV, 15—Wherefore glorify ye the Lord in the fires.

The character we bear and the position we occupy, form, jointly, an unmistakable index to our duty. We are offenders against God, and we belong to a race of offenders; and hence we are bound to humble ourselves, and to endeavour to reclaim others. We are always liable to suffer, and the world in which we live is full of suffering; and hence a reason why we should cultivate a spirit of patience and trust, of sympathy and benevolence. We live under the government of an infinitely good and gracious God, and there is not an hour, even in the darkest night of adversity, when we are not sharing the tokens of his bounty; and this feature of our condition surely demands our unceasing gratitude and praise. These several dispositions, forming the leading elements of Christian character, are not to be cultivated as if each was an insulated quality, independent of the rest,—but in harmonious combination ; while yet the circumstances in which we are placed, must determine which of them, at any given time, is to be brought more immediately into exercise.

The general truth which I have here stated, has, if I mistake not, a striking illustration in the present condition of our country ; and I might, with equal ease, and equal propriety, derive from it an argument for the cultivation of any of those inward feelings, or the performance of any of those outward acts, to which I have referred. I might very reasonably call upon you, as a part of this great nation, to humble yourselves before God for that crimson guilt which has so long been challenging the Divine justice, and has now brought us into circumstances of such fearful jeopardy. Or I might address myself more immediately to your benevolent feelings—I might invoke your sympathy and prayers for the multitudes, North and South, who are weeping bitterly to-day in their desolate homes, because those whom they loved most have fallen in battle ; or I might invoke your charity in aid of the brave soldiers who have gone to do our work,

and who will soon be encountering the blasts
of winter, and some of whom, I may add, are
already suffering from diseases or wounds; or I
might invoke the exercise of a considerate and
forgiving spirit towards our brethren with
whom we are in conflict,—the mass of whom
we believe to be acting under an honest
delusion. But the circumstances in which we
are assembled, while they do not exclude any
of these subjects from our contemplation, but
rather bring them before us, at least indirectly,
yet point our thoughts mainly in the direction
of mercies received. And this is in full
accordance with the Proclamation of our
honoured Chief Magistrate, which I have just
read to you.

To *glorify God* is to use our faculties in
obedience to his will, and in honour of his
perfections. To glorify God *in the fires* is to
cherish the right dispositions, and perform the
fitting actions, in the time of trouble. We
glorify Him when we bow quietly, patiently,
trustingly, before his righteous hand. We
glorify Him when our spirits grow familiar with
Heaven, as we take fresh lessons in the furnace.
We glorify Him by using the means, which

affliction may bring with it, of doing good to those around us. And, finally, we glorify Him in a thankful acknowledgement of the mercies which mingle with our afflictions, and qualify their severity, and of the benevolent ends, in respect to both ourselves and others, which we can see, in the distance, as having been accomplished through our suffering. Hence the propriety of keeping a Day of Thanksgiving now, when the political heavens are giving forth nothing but storm and hail; when the whole nation is writhing and struggling because the iron is piercing her heart.

The return of this anniversary, as has been very properly intimated in the Proclamation, finds us in quiet possession of a large part of our accustomed blessings. We, especially, who live at a distance from the scene of conflict, are hardly sensible of any diminution of our means of enjoyment, except as we necessarily share the suspense and agitation incident to our near relation to those events which are electrifying the whole world. If we look into our dwellings, we find our tables as bounteously spread, and our domestic relations fraught with as manifold blessings, as ever. If we extend

our views into the community to which we
more immediately belong, we witness the
general prevalence of peace, and health, and
industry, and mutual confidence. If we think
of our religious privileges, we find that they
are in no wise diminished; and if we send our
thoughts abroad, where the missionaries were
doing their Lord's work on the last Thanksgiving Day, we shall see them engaged still, as
busily, and cheerfully, and successfully, as
ever. These are all blessings which may now,
and at any time, very properly come up in
thankful remembrance before God; but, in this
discourse, I am going to take you into the very
midst of the fires, to find the material for your
gratitude to work upon; and I shall hope to
show you that it is a benevolent as well as a
just God who is moving in all this darkness;
that in the events we deplore, there is something besides bitterness, and terror, and death;
and that it becometh us to wait, in thankful
expectation, for that jubilee which shall crown
the lifting away of the cloud. Let me then
suggest several GROUNDS OF THANKSGIVING con-
nected with that general state of things, which
we so earnestly deprecated in the prospect, and

2

which is so deeply fraught with present calamity.

I. The conflict in which we are engaged, has brought into vigorous, unquestionable exercise that spirit of *lofty patriotism*, which had slumbered so long that its very existence had begun to be doubted. It is a law of human nature that we come gradually to undervalue those blessings which we never see put in jeopardy. These goodly institutions, under whose shadow we have reposed so long, had their foundation in the labours, the sacrifices, the very blood, of our fathers; and the world never saw a purer, nobler patriotism than that by which they were animated. These men, as long as they lived, kept the fire glowing, not only in their own bosoms, but in their children's also; but since nearly all of them have passed away, and our memories are no longer refreshed by the personal recital of their heroic sufferings and exploits, there is reason to fear that our appreciation of the inheritance they have bequeathed to us has lost somewhat both of vividness and of gratitude. And there has been yet another adverse influence at work,— that of political partisanship—men of different factions, in their regard for minor, perhaps personal, interests,—possibly for the mere indulgence of passion or the triumph of self-will, have suggested, originated, or sanctioned measures of dangerous, if not fatal, bearing upon our national prosperity. The result of all this has been, as might be expected, that the public mind has become darkened; the public conscience defiled; the public heart hardened; and whether or not the spirit of true patriotism must not suffer from such a process as this, judge ye. It *has* suffered,—insomuch that many wise and good men have believed that they were walking over its grave. It was not dead after all; and yet it required an almost miraculous energy to revivify and re-establish it, and put it once more to its appropriate work. One year ago, when we assembled on the occasion of this anniversary, we felt that the general warring of the political elements among ourselves cast a dark shadow over us—the harsh murmurs of party spirit grated upon our ear; and it seemed as if the altar was preparing on which our national liberty was to be offered up. To-day, we do not indeed see all the political parties merged in a common mass,—and I do not believe that would be a thing even to be desired;—for men are most likely to do right when they know that there are some watching to see if they do wrong—but in regard to the question whether the great political fabric which our fathers built, shall stand or fall; whether we shall make an inglorious surrender of all that we hold dear as a nation, or cling to it at the sacrifice of our blood;—I am sure that if there are any who even falter at this point, they take care to give utterance to their views in the night, and then speak only in whispers. And it is refreshing to mark the history of the revival of the patriotic spirit. It slept, or at best was in doubtful exercise, amidst the plottings and even the ravings of party, for several months after the terrible engine, designed to crush our liberties, began to show itself; and even those who were ready to stand by their country, in any emergency, and at any hazard, were obliged to look at that instrument of destruction for a long time before they could be persuaded that their eyes were in contact with an actual reality. But the bombardment of Fort Sumter, followed by the bloody scenes in

the streets of Baltimore, cured us all of our
incredulity in respect to the doom to which a
portion of our countrymen had adjudged us.
We saw, we felt, then, for the first time, that
we had certainly reached a point of imminent
peril ; and that the question we had to settle
was whether the nation should live or die.
And then it was that the patriotic fires burst
forth on every side of us ; in high places
and in low places; from the bosoms of men
of opposite parties ;—constituting a glorious
pledge that all minor questions of policy should
be postponed until the one great question,
involving our national existence, should be
determined.

But was not this the mere effect of a surprise ;
an effervescence of feeling, which would die
away with the occasion that immediately pro-
duced it ? Perhaps, in view of the acknowledged
elasticity of our national character, we should
have had no reason to complain if such a question had been asked when the great impulse
to the public mind was first communicated ; but
it is too late to ask it now; for history has
already anticipated the answer. That universal
involuntary movement, that formed the august

response to the barbarous attack on Sumter, inaugurated a new and better condition of the public mind: the intense excitement, thus originated, gradually settled into a calm and earnest purpose; and the whole loyal heart of the country pledged itself for the preservation of our Union. The President, by his Proclamation, convened Congress—and a nobly patriotic body it was—a few indeed, by their treasonable deliverances, sought to produce discord in the otherwise harmonious deliberations, thus fixing upon themselves a mark of infamy that will last when every other memorial of them has perished. But, with these humiliating exceptions, Congress,—though still consisting of two parties which had been sternly arrayed against each other,—yet moved on in the majesty of a substantially united body, responding to the calls of the President with a promptness and an alacrity that all posterity will honour. They authorized the raising of an army fully adequate to the emergency; and they provided, as far as they could provide, the requisite pecuniary means for prosecuting the war; and then it only remained for the people to say whether they should be met in hearty and vigorous co-operation. The process of voluntary enlistment began at once in all the loyal States, and has been going on ever since; the mere stripling, and the man of gray hairs, has each claimed it as a right to fight for his country; and now, after the lapse of a little more than seven months, more than six hundred thousand men are actually in the field, or are ready to enter it. And, as for money, not only were the treasures of Wall Street proffered to the Government with a freedom which knew no limit, but many of the more prominent monied institutions in our large cities offered themselves as auxiliaries for carrying on the war. We should have expected, beforehand, that, in a majority of cases at least, parental or conjugal or filial love would have sighed over, if it had not actually protested against, the departure of the nearest kindred on an errand of so much uncertainty and peril; but, instead of that, we hear, on every side, of mothers and wives and daughters, bidding good cheer to those most dear to them, even when they cannot resist the impression that they may be parting to meet no more. And I may say, in this connection, that the very nobility of patriotism is constantly displayed by our women. The newspapers are, almost every week, reporting to us the presentation, by ladies of the highest rank, of splendid banners to military companies;—banners on which the Stars and Stripes, gloriously displayed, bear witness that, even if the men should falter, the female heart of the nation would still be all right. And there is yet another testimony, of the same import, in the use to which the sewing machine is put, in many a dwelling, for providing our brave soldiers with comfortable garments, and especially in those truly honourable gatherings, in which the high and the low, the rich and the poor, work together, and then blend the fruits of their labour in one common patriotic offering. And as I have spoken of the women, I will speak of the children also—for the military air and badges with which they appear, marching about the streets, is significant—it shows that Patriotism has become domesticated in our dwellings, so as to give complexion to the sports and diversions even of our little ones.

I should be unjust to my own sense of duty, if I were not, in connection with what I am now saying, to render a distinct tribute to some of the illustrious men, whose names are most closely and most honourably interwoven with the pending enterprise. There is already a pretty long list of martyrs to this cause; prominent among whom are ELLSWORTH, and WINTHROP, and GREBLE, and WARD, and LYON, and BAKER—these and many others, who have poured out their blood as a free-will offering to their country, deserve a lasting memorial; and, as sure as there is gratitude in the American heart, they shall have it. The memory of DOUGLASS, too, Patriotism will ever cherish; for though he died not on the battle field, and lived not to witness any thing beyond the earliest stage of the conflict, yet the utterances even of his death-bed were a lesson to the nation, on the great duty of self-preservation, which she has already embalmed in her inmost heart. And then to come to the living—I will say nothing of those who occupy the highest places in the government, except that the party who would gladly have prevented their being placed there, are now not only generally tolerant of their measures, but actually meet them in a spirit of generous confidence and co-operation—and more or

3

better than this I could not wish to say.
Among those whose patriotic eloquence has
most effectually enlightened and thrilled the
masses in different parts of our country, are
HOLT, and EVERETT, and DICKINSON; each of
whom has hereby established a fresh claim
upon the gratitude and admiration of posterity.
MCCLELLAN and WOOL, ANDERSON, DIX and SHER-
MAN, may very well represent the great spirits
of our Army; and DUPONT and WILKES, of
our Navy—yes, *Wilkes*, even though we were
to admit, as we do not, that the legality of the
act that has immortalized him, is still an open
question. Some of our Ex-Presidents, it is
well known, have their hearts fully in the great
national movement, and, in their dignified re-
tirement, are counselling to energetic and decisive measures; and one of them, an honoured
inhabitant of our own State,* does not disdain
to appear weekly in a soldier's uniform, and
drill a military company. CRITTENDEN, too,
Kentucky's venerable statesman, who laboured
so long, so honestly, and yet so ineffectually,
for compromise, instead of showing a pitiful
resentment that his counsels were not heeded,
by refusing all co-operation with those from

*Mr. Fillmore.

whom he differed, has shown himself as mag-
nanimous as he is patriotic—his great mind
and great heart are both fully enlisted in the
service of his country ; and his noble son, with
sword in hand, represents him on the field.
And if I were to undertake to add to this list
the names of those who have been, and still are,
serving their country, by means of the pen, I
should present to you a host, made up of not a
small portion of our most gifted minds—I
should repeat a multitude of honoured names,
which are as household words in the walks of
American literature ; and among them the
name of PARSON BROWNLOW would certainly have
a place, though, if the latest accounts may be re-
lied on, it seems doubtful whether his pen or his
sword is to win for him his brightest honours.
In short, Patriotism has had her well trained
agents in all the various spheres of public activ-
ity.   She directs the thoughts and purposes of
those who fill our stations of influence and
honour.   She moves among the masses, like a
good angel in white robes.   She breathes light
and hope into the darkness of the hour.   And
who will not say that her presence is to be acknowledged as a blessing from on high ?   Should

we not greatly come short of the appropriate duties of this day, if we should fail to give God thanks that Patriotism has no longer a dubious existence here, but is displaying herself in decisive, far-reaching, mighty manifestations ?

II. Another ground of thanksgiving, in connection with the events of the day is, that *we are permitted to live in a period of such surpassing interest.* But I hear you ask whether the exact opposite of this is not true ; and whether the sentiment I am now putting forth, does not contradict the whole tenor of a discourse, in which, not long since, I endeavoured to show you that the great and good spirits, who were then passing away, were mercifully taken from the evil to come. I answer, the statement in that discourse, and the position which I now assume, are in perfect harmony. The explanation of the apparent discrepancy is, that it is a mixed state of things with which we have to do; that bright events have their dark side, and dark events have their bright side ; and that the same event, in different aspects, may be fraught with both calamity and blessing. The war now in progress brings with it terrible scenes of distress and desola-

tion ; and we cannot but pronounce those highly
favoured who have escaped them by being
called up to Heaven ; but it is no less true that
the war is a great school which God Himself
has opened for the improvement of the living—
there are lessons given here, in relation not
only to the deep things of the human heart,
but the great principles of the Divine government, fitted to enlarge our views and exalt our
characters, and which ought, therefore, to be
received with thankfulness and praise.

If the scenes through which we are passing
be contemplated as a mere matter of *curiosity*,
(and this is the least important view we can
take of them,) we shall find that they possess
an interest not often paralleled in human expe-
rience. Curiosity, or the desire of knowledge,
is among the original principles of our nature;
and wherever you find human beings, there
you see its operation. How men will cross
oceans, and climb mountains, and traverse
deserts, and imperil their lives, merely to behold the wonders of nature, or, as the case
may be, to stand on the spot rendered memo-
rable by some signal event in history ! What
an oracle every living relic of the Revolution

is at this day ! How eagerly we question him in respect to all that he saw, and heard, and felt, during that dark period ; and how his very presence renders more impressive the events that are perfectly familiar to us ! And when, aided by the light of history, we go back a little farther ; when we pause amidst the stirring scenes of the old French and Indian wars, or amidst the fearful perils and trials that attended the first settlement of our country; or when we penetrate yet deeper into the past, and read of the destruction of Jerusalem by the Romans, and its more ancient destruction by the Chaldeans, and of the circumstances which attended, and the consequences that followed, the siege, in each case, are we not half inclined to wish that we might have seen with our own eyes these signal wonders that history has reported to us? We are thankful for the record ; but we cannot help feeling how much more minute would have been our knowledge, and how much more impressive the facts, if we could have actually witnessed what we now receive only on testimony. I do not say that the events, now taking place among ourselves, will ever rank in the same category with those just referred to, as marking the grand epochs of Jewish history; and I do not say that they will *not;* for there is some reason to believe that they are introductory to a new stage in human affairs— but certainly here is a field in which the most intense curiosity finds itself gratified and rewarded; in which the most inveterate lovers of the marvellous and the startling may expatiate indefinitely, and yet be finding some fresh wonder every day. Will not our children, whose memories are taking in these grand and terrible occurrences, if they should live threescore or fourscore years, think it a privilege to have been the witnesses of what is now passing; and will not the generation that succeeds them, sit reverently in their presence, to hear of the great things of which they will then be the only living depositaries?

It is not, however, merely or chiefly the gratification of curiosity that constitutes the advantage of living at this period; but, as I have just intimated, Providence is now most impressively urging upon our consideration *certain great moral truths,* having respect to our danger and our duty, to man and to God, which are eminently adapted to improve and elevate our characters. Let me hint at a few of them.

I say, then, the great rebellion, now in progress, furnishes, in the conduct of its *leaders,* a striking illustration of *the madness of human ambition.* When the first demonstration of revolt was made, I confess I believed, and I presume most of us believed, that it was an honest, though sadly unjustifiable, measure of retaliation for what we were generally willing to acknowledge was an unreasonable interference, on the part of certain Northern men, with the peculiar institution of the South; or that, if the evil complained of was more extensive than this, it was a supposed general diseased state of the Northern mind in relation to the same subject. But a speech from a distinguished member of Congress from Pennsylvania,* which has since been substantially reproduced in various public documents, convinced me, as I doubt not it did many others, that the rebellion which had then been formally proclaimed, had another and a deeper cause than Northern Abolitionism. That speech proved, beyond a peradventure, that it was no unpremeditated movement that Carolina was then

* Hon. Edward McPherson.

making; that it was the carrying out of a carefully matured plan;—a plan having for its object nothing less than the dissolution of the Union, which their and our fathers had constituted, and the establishment of a new empire, probably after some transatlantic model. It was clearly because these men were disgusted with the levelling workings of our republican system, and wanted something more congenial with the tastes and habits of Aristocracy, that they ventured on the desperate experiment now in progress. It was this that made them repudiate the obligations of a most solemn compact; that lifted the State into an attitude of defiance against her whole loyal sisterhood; that spread the spirit of revolt from State to State, till it seemed as if the little leaven would leaven the whole lump; and that has now changed what was intended to be the theatre of its own triumph into a terrible field of devastation and slaughter. Did ever ambition accomplish for itself a more hateful, a more profitless, a more fatal work? Does not every deserted village, every threatened city, every booming cannon, every soldier's grave, charge madness upon those whose unholy aspirations for power have

4

thus turned beauty into deformity, prosperity into calamity, life into death ?

Again : This rebellion, so far as respects the *masses*, is a wonderful instance of *the workings of an extended popular delusion.* Sadly do they misunderstand the actual state of things, who believe that the people of the South, as a body, are false to their own convictions, in engaging in this conflict. They have been trained to believe that nearly the whole North are bitterly hostile to them, and are resolved that their slaves shall be set free, even though it be at the expense of a re-enactment of the bloody scenes of St. Domingo. And is it strange that, with such impressions, they should cheerfully follow the bidding of their leaders, in vindication of what they believe to be their own rights ? Is it strange that, in the faith of such a Proclamation as Beauregard made at Manassas, they should address themselves with lion-like courage, even with tiger-like ferocity, to the bloody work of retaliation ? Are you quite sure that, if you were to change places with them, and to have the veil over your eyes as it is over theirs, you would not follow in their footsteps, even to the work of death ? A large part of all the evil committed in the world is to be referred to the influence of delusion. Men have only to put darkness for light,—to work themselves into the belief of a lie, and then carry out their own honest convictions, to render themselves the scourges of society,—as the case may be, to spread desolation over a Continent. We can pity the victims of popular delusion, but the authors of it the whole world view with abhorrence.

Again: In the startling events of the day we may see *what a mighty energy there is in the human will*, especially when viewed in connection with a widely extended sympathy and co-operation. All great achievements, so far as they are the result of human agency, have brought into vigorous exercise the mind's power of determination; not excepting even those cases in which the Providence of God interposes to bring about a different end from that which the projectors of the enterprise had contemplated. One year ago, though there were indeed dark clouds visible in our political horizon, yet those who profess to be wise in such matters, told us that they were mere flying, harmless clouds, that would quickly disappear.

We knew that many of our Southern brethren had been alienated from us, and most of us were willing to acknowledge that some of their complaints were not without cause ; but we felt that the tie which bound them and us together, was too sacred not to be indissoluble. Then we had no army that deserved the name. The few ships we had, which were only an apology for a navy, had nearly all gone off, strangely enough, into distant oceans. Our citizens were quietly pursuing their respective vocations, without molestation and without apprehension. The intercourse between the North and the South was constant and unembarrassed. And so firmly were we convinced of the substantial unity of the nation, that, when decisive signs of disruption began to appear, we were slow to admit even the testimony of our senses. But, since that period, eleven States have abjured their allegiance to the Government, and boldly set up for themselves. More than a million of men have abandoned their accustomed occupations, and rushed exultingly to the perils of a soldier's life. Our few scattered ships have been recalled for domestic service, and have proved the nucleus of an already efficient navy.

Terrible battles have been fought,—victories
have been won, and defeats encountered, on
both sides. And the history of the world may
be challenged for a grander, more imposing,
more appalling picture than our country presents to-day. And all this has been accomplished within much less than a year, by the
energy of the human will! May not this very
reasonably exalt our conceptions of the dignity
of our nature? Who will not bow reverently
before his own spirit, in consideration of its
possessing an attribute that lifts it into such
immediate alliance with Divinity?

Again: It would be difficult to find a
more striking illustration than this rebellion
presents, of *the well-nigh boundless capabilities of
human depravity.* What an offence against God
and man was involved in that first thought
in which the rebellion had its origin; in the
maturing of the thought into a plan; in the
development of the plan into open and horrible
acts! Herein God's command to be subject to
the powers that be was trampled upon; while
the highest obligations of truth and justice
towards man were outraged in the attempt to
overthrow a government, which promised more

of blessing to the world than any other. Such a plan as this, we should know, beforehand, could be accomplished only by means of the foulest treachery—and now that the mists in which the plan was conceived and carried forward, are cleared away, we are met with the revolting revelation that it has been nursed by men who sat in our halls of National Legislation, and in the high places of our Government, and who were meanly receiving from the United States' treasury, from eight to twenty-one dollars a day, for grinding the axe by which they expected that the fair fabric of our Union was to be hewed in pieces. And the conflict which was begun in treachery, has been marked, in its progress, by barbarity, unequalled in the annals of civilized warfare. Witness the deliberate torturing to death of some of the poor captives at Manassas; and the perfectly fiend-like demonstration by which our troops were butchered in the village of Guyandotte; and, more recently, the officially proclaimed threat that, if the law in relation to piracy, which we have in common with all civilized nations, is suffered to take its course, then one of our brave officers whom they hold in captivity, and have already immured in a felon's cell, shall expiate the crime of the Government, and wipe out the dishonour done to the Chivalry, amidst the horrors of the gallows. And last of all, Carolina, boasting and would-be bloody Carolina, is gravely, or rather madly, proposing to set the black flag, that terrible emblem of unsparing slaughter, waving in all her borders. Verily, these demonstrations, though coming only in the form of threats, must curdle the blood of the whole civilized world !

I say, these are terrible exhibitions of human depravity ; but truth and fairness require me to add that much of guilt also, in connection with the prosecution of this war, lies at *our* door. One crime that is patent to the whole world is falsehood. So unscrupulous is the Telegraph, which represents, I fear, but too faithfully, the state of the public conscience, that, when good tidings come, we have learned to suppress our joy, and when bad tidings come, we have learned to keep down our grief, until some two or three confirmatory messages have reached us. Not only is this a great evil in itself,—a gross offence against both God and man, but it has already been productive of much positive disaster to the country, besides strengthening the hands of evil doers, and generating a vast amount of needless apprehension. I may mention also the reckless disregard of private rights and private property, which has been manifested, here and there, by our soldiers; though these wayward and destructive tendencies have, I believe, generally met with a stern rebuke from the proper military authorities. And there is yet another form which our iniquity has assumed,—I mean that of gross dishonesty in public contracts,—speculating on the woes of the country,—giving to the poor soldiers, who are imperilling every thing for us, wooden-soled shoes, and flimsy, half-made garments, instead of the substantial articles that were bargained for. Such conduct has in it the elements of meanness and cruelty as well as perfidy. They who are chargeable with it, had better leave it to others to expatiate upon the guilt, and determine the deserts, of traitors.

I say then, my friends, whether you look at the North or the South, you see that this war is uncovering and rendering palpable the very

depths of human depravity. It is indeed a
shocking spectacle to contemplate, and one
which calls us to the deepest humiliation; but
it suggests counsel, warning, instruction, which
cannot but do us good, if we lay it suitably to
heart, and which may very properly, therefore,
come into our remembrance on a Thanksgiving
Day.

Again: The rebellion furnishes a striking
illustration of the *silent growth of evil*. That
gigantic evil, with which the nation is now
struggling, I may safely say, had a small beginning—possibly it began in deep silence, and
amidst doubts, and conflicts, and gloomy fore-
bodings, which it took much time and much
hard dealing with the conscience to get rid of.
I suppose it is generally admitted that the
terrible movement was inaugurated, more than
thirty years ago, by a great Southern politi-
cian;—a man of comprehensive and powerful
intellect, of fine social qualities, and every way
unexceptionable in private life, but still possessing insatiable ambition and boundless obsti-
nacy. His first demonstrations in favour of
disunion were met by a spirit and a hand that
awed the treasonable policy, not indeed out of

5

existence, but into comparative silence. I do not wish to utter harsh words over any man's grave, or to heap odium on the memories of those who have gone to render their account— I cannot tell in what false lights that great man of whom I speak may have looked at his favourite project, and, as the result, fancied that he could justify it to his conscience; but I do say that, if tradition deals justly with him, it was in *his* bosom that that serpent, whose deadly fangs have now struck into the very heart of our republic, was generated. At first, it was insensible, impalpable, unacknowledged; but still there was life in it,—a life that was essentially venomous; and it kept gradually gaining strength until the creature began to move. And, as the years passed away, it gathered nourishment from other hearts than that in which it was born; and a spirit of officious ultraism at the North contributed materially to its growth; until, at length, the day came when it worked its way fully out of its hiding place, and stretched itself, to the full extent of its dimensions, across the land,—a huge monster, combining the poison of the viper with the boa-constrictor's crushing power. And now, for months, it has been showing us its tongue of fire, and hissing out its bitter threats, and making a desperate effort to infold the whole nation in its deadly coils. I trust in God there is a spirit awake, before which, with all its virulence and strength, it will be obliged to quail; but, meanwhile, it shows more impressively than words can do, not only how the spirit of evil chooses the darkness as its appropriate element, but how it sometimes accomplishes wonders before its existence even has been fairly detected. What a lesson of warning is here to note vigilantly the signs of the times, and to keep ourselves in an attitude for resisting evil, whenever, wherever, or however, it may manifest itself!

I only add, under this branch of my subject, that the current events are bringing out *the character of God*, in some of its aspects, no less clearly than the character of man. God rules the world by fixed laws; and the danger is that the uniformity of their operation will make men oblivious of both his agency and his presence. Hence it is that, though these laws are always in force, working out their proper results, yet to rebuke the tendencies to practical atheism, which exist in many minds, God is pleased, sometimes, in the administration of his government, to come forth from the hiding-place of his power, clothed in unwonted majesty and terror. How manifest is it that, in the scenes through which we are now passing, He is turning towards us some of the more awful aspects of his character! Do we not feel that we are in contact with the retributive justice of God; that, though He has borne with us long, He has at length come out in judgment against us for our iniquities, while yet He tempers judgment with mercy? That such a fearful conflict as this should have arisen, when we had begun to look out for the dawn of the millenial age,—and arisen here, on ground which had been consecrated by the presence of a pure Christianity for more than two centuries; that this nation, after attaining a glorious manhood, should stand forth before the world as a house divided against itself, exhibiting the strangely revolting spectacle of men thirsting, even to desperation, for the blood of brothers;--that such a state of things should exist, I say, is a testimony, visible, palpable, that clouds and darkness are round about Jehovah's Throne. Events have already occurred, too, in the progress of the war, which have shown that it is God's province, not only to bring light out of darkness, but to render evil the minister of good. I doubt not that we have far more to be thankful for to-day, than we should have had but for some things that have made our hearts burn with indignation, or bleed with bitter grief. When, too, we bear in mind that this vast and complicated machinery, which is now at work, all over this land, with such mighty power, is all directed by Him who sitteth in the Heavens, for the accomplishment of purposes which his own infinite wisdom has devised, can we forbear to exclaim, in the fulness of an humble and reverential spirit,— "Who is so great a God as our God!"

Has not enough been said to justify my position that there are certain aspects of this dark day that make it a privilege to live in it? Is it not a day when God's utterances to this nation are louder and more impressive than they ever were before? Is it not a desirable thing to live when there are such unprecedented advantages for studying the human heart; when God comes so near to us that we cannot but feel his terrible, and yet gracious, presence ; when the lessons He inculcates are at once identified with, and enforced by, the discipline He inflicts, and both are on a scale so grand and awful as to overawe every thoughtful and reverent spirit? Truly, we do not mistake in reckoning this among the legitimate subjects of our thanksgiving.

III. As another ground for thankfulness to-day, I may mention the fact—and I appeal to you to say whether it is *not* a fact—that, while we are constrained to regard a large portion of our Southern brethren, at present, as enemies, *there is no prevailing hostility towards them in the North*—if I understand the feeling, it is a strong sense of the criminality of the leaders, but a disposition to make large allowance for the masses, on the ground that they have been deceived by false representations; while we would gladly welcome them all back to their allegiance, without asking for any humiliating concessions, or seeking to add to the burdens which they have so recklessly assumed. It certainly cannot be denied that we are accustomed to speak of their hostile demonstrations

in terms of strong disapproval; particularly that
some of our newspapers, in making their deliverances concerning them, are not over-careful
to choose out the softest words—it could not
be otherwise, unless the legitimate workings of
human nature, even as it exists in good men,
were suspended—nevertheless, I greatly mistake, if the general tone of Northern feeling
towards the South is even allied to malignity
or revenge. We will not indeed be so kind-
hearted as to look on coolly, and make no re-
sistance, while they are rushing forward in
their present mad career—the very graves of
our fathers would reproach us if we should re-
fuse the sacrifice even of our blood, for the
maintainance of those institutions which it
cost *their* blood to establish. But we require
nothing at their hands, but that they fall back
into the position in which they were placed by
that sacred league which they cannot violate,
without insulting the memories of a galaxy of
illustrious patriots, whose names constitute the
pride of their own history. I know there are
a few among us, who would violate the Constitution in one way, as *they* would violate it in
another ; that is, who would move for an in-

stantaneous and universal emancipation of their slaves, regardless of the fearful consequences that must ensue. But no such fanatical delusion as this has got possession of the Northern mind. Whatever rights the Constitution accords to them, we hold ourselves bound to respect, except in so far as the necessities of the war into which they have plunged us, may require that they should be infringed. Most of us have friends scattered through the South, and some of us, in nearly every disloyal State,—who, either from conviction, or from the pressure of circumstances, are following the multitude : much as we regret their position, we have kind and grateful thoughts of them still; and, if there should be an opportunity for the renewal of our intercourse with them, I am sure they would be as welcome to the hospitalities of our dwellings, and to any good services we could render them, as if no disruption had occurred. Such I verily believe to be the pervading tone of Northern feeling at this stage of the conflict; and I leave it to you to decide whether this is not one of the things that ought to come into remembrance on this Thanksgiving Day. .

IV. In the review of *what has been already accomplished, looking towards our ultimate success in this great struggle,* we find another cause of thankfulness to our Divine Benefactor.

We cannot estimate this consideration aright, without taking into view the actual state of things, when the rebellion began to take on a palpable form. Had there been any preparation made by our Government for holding her property against the ruthless hand of domestic invasion? Had she taken care to husband her resources with prudent reference to being ready for an attack; and, when the tocsin of war was sounded, had she nothing to do but to respond, by her hundreds of thousands of well armed men, ready to take the field? So far from it, her own energies and resources had been perverted to prepare for making the attack, instead of acting on the defence; and, when her traitorous agents threw off the mask, they evidently felt bold and strong in the conviction that they had little else to do than to appropriate and enjoy the fruits of their perfidious labours. Their successors in office were slow to believe even what their eyes saw; and the measure of their indulgence, honourable as

6

it may have been to their generous feelings, had well-nigh overtaxed the patience of the nation. But, at length, the fearful emergency glared upon them, so that they were not only convinced of the obligation, but shut up to the necessity, of vigorous effort; and from that period may be said to date the commencement of a course of preparation for the conflict, which, for its rapidity, and extent, and thoroughness, may be safely pronounced to be without parallel in the history of the world. What it is I need not attempt to tell you—suffice it to say, it is a prodigious military and naval power, that is ready to be called into exercise whenever and wherever there is an exigency to require it. And more than that,—this power is constantly increasing; and still more,—the fountain from which it flows is inexhaustible.

But it is not merely the fact that our Government has made such formidable preparations for attack and defence in so short a time, and that, too, against all the obstacles which Treason had been able to set up,—that calls for our gratitude ; but it is the additional fact that she has entered vigorously upon her work

of crushing the power that has set her authority
at defiance. I should only recite the current
events of the day, if I were to go into details on
this subject; but it will occur to you, at once,
that there are one or two strongholds, within the
bounds of the self-styled Confederacy, which
have never passed into their possession, whose
terrible frown falls upon the whole surround-
ing country like the shadow of death. You
will remember, too, how nobly Maryland—to
say nothing of Kentucky—has already been
saved to the Union; and *that* because the brave
and patriotic Dix knew how to strangle Treason as well as to direct the use of artillery.
You will think how manfully Western Vir-
ginia has withstood the storm that was pelting
her, declaring her allegiance to the Nation
at the expense of dissolving her connection
with the State; and now we have tidings that
some of the Eastern counties, upon which the
light of the admirable Proclamation from Fort
McHenry has fallen, are moving in the same
track. You will think of the victory at
Hatteras Inlet, by which a ball was set in
motion, that has rolled so fast and so far
already, that the Stars and Stripes are floating

over large portions of North Carolina. And
the yet later, and far more important victory,
at Port Royal, will, I am sure, come gratefully
into your thoughts ;—a victory that has planted
our National Flag on ground where it was dis-
honoured first; which secures greater advantages to our cause than could have been gained
at almost any other point, and which must be
like a dark sign in the heavens to those who
are watching to see the American Eagle die.
And last of all, I am sure you will not fail to
remember (for it must have been in your
thoughts ever since it occurred) that heroic
adventure of the Naval Commander WILKES,
by which two rebel emissaries were waylaid,
on their mission to foreign lands, and brought
to breathe the air, and behold the faces, which
they hated most; thus defeating purposes of
mischief, and making it perhaps a little more
difficult to carry out the bloody threat in respect to Corcoran, and his brave associates in
captivity. I only hint at these main facts,
and leave it to your memory to supply the
rest; but I am sure you will agree with me
that a sober review of the history of the last
seven months brings before us many tokens of

the Divine favour, in our actual success, which it becomes us gratefully to acknowledge.

But I hear some one say that this is but a one-sided representation of our case — it is alleged that these are only a few bright spots in a generally dark picture; or, at best, that we have had too many disheartening reverses, mortifying defeats, to justify any great exultation in view of our success. My first reply to this unpatriotic suggestion is, that war must always have its chances; that, as it is conducted by imperfect men, however sagacious or brave they may be, there can be no security against occasional mistakes, that may seem temporarily to jeopard even the best cause. Then again, who does not perceive that the great disadvantage, on our part, under which the war was entered upon, was almost sure, in its earlier stages, to put to a severe test our faith in the ultimate triumph of our cause? And, finally, while the defeats and embarrassments which we have actually encountered, have been no greater than we had a right to expect, they have only helped to strengthen the nation's heart; and we have causes for thanksgiving this morning, which we should not have had but for that dark and bloody day, which a portion of our army spent at Manassas. That there may have been errors of judgment in the conduct of the war, nobody will question ; but I submit to you whether, considering the vastness of the enterprise, the variety and complication of the interests involved, the fearful odds against which Treason and Rebellion had to be met, we have not far more reason to testify of mercy than of judgment; of success than of defeat.

V. Once more : If the past furnishes ground for thanksgiving, not less, surely, does *the prospect that opens upon us.* I say this in full view of the fact that the future is, to a great extent, hid in the bosom of Omniscience ; and that events which, by reason of our shortsightedness, we call contingencies, sometimes, temporarily at least, give a different direction to the general course of affairs from what we had desired and expected. Hence we are not to be disappointed if, in the progress of the conflict, there should be other reverses still in store for us, that will make even the most hopeful and jubilant feel, for the moment, like hanging their harps upon the willows. But, after making all due allowance for the uncertainty that necessarily pertains to the future, I cannot but think that the signs of the times are so decidedly auspicious as to forbid all doubt that the contest will finally issue in the full re-establishment of our Union. On the question, how soon this grand result may be reached, or how many cities may be sacked, or how many fields drenched in blood, before it shall be reached, the most far-seeing may well suppress even their conjectures; but that our struggle is to find its end in this, seems to me scarcely less certain than that the order of nature will proceed.

If I mistake not, there were many of us who had grown so tired of the clamour of the South against the North and the North against the South, who had become so sick of reading Congressional Speeches steeped in gall, and especially of reading of such horrible facts as the raid of John Brown and his associates, and the doom which so speedily overtook them, that we were ready to say even,— "Let the quarrel be terminated by a peaceful division of the Union." But, if we said this, as I know some of us did, it was an impatient and hasty judgment which a little reflection corrected. For we saw at once that the geographical position of the country forbade a division ; that the very mountains and rivers lifted up their voice against it; that the immense tract between the Atlantic and Pacific Oceans, between our great Lakes and the Gulf of Mexico, had been determined, by Him who fixes the bounds of our habitation, to be the natural home of one vast united people. And it is equally obvious that, while no limit can be fixed to the amount of blessing which such a nation, united, can procure for itself, and diffuse through the world, its division could be the harbinger of nothing but evil;—evil to itself, inasmuch as the separate States or Districts into which it would fall, would exhaust their energies in mutual jealousies leading to bitter conflicts ; evil to the rest of the world, as it would extinguish the last hope of a Republican Government, and put more iron into the heart and the arm of every despot under heaven. In view of these considerations, the loyal States have decided,—calmly and solemnly decided, that the Union shall not be broken ; that, by God's blessing, the machinations of those who are plotting to bring about this mighty evil, shall be defeated. This purpose is declared in the sudden fading out, in a great measure, of party lines; in the alacrity, the magnanimity, with which men, great men, of different political creeds, are seen rushing to the common rescue. And the purpose will be carried out;—yes, carried out to the very letter;—for the spirit that has decreed it, you may chain when you can chain the rushing tempest; or you may bribe, when you can bribe the angel that watches about you. What meaneth this vast army that has been brought together under an almost magical impulse; while it has left behind the material for another, and yet another, army like it,—equally brave, equally patriotic, equally powerful; which it would require only the announcement of the exigency, to mould into form, and bring into the field? What meaneth it that, when the veteran and venerable Commander-in-Chief retired, bearing with him the laurels he had been gathering for more than half a century, there was found among us a youthful hero, whom Providence had schooled to receive his mantle and take his place;—a man as thought-

7

ful, and far-seeing, and modest withal, as he is
brave;—a man who had scarcely taken his military position before he threw up a grand en-
trenchment around the Holy Sabbath, and who
mingles with his wisely adjusted and thoroughly
matured plans, devout acknowledgements of
his dependence on a Higher Power; and, I may
add, a man who commands the perfect confidence, not only of the army and the country at
large, but—what is certainly remarkable—of
his own senior associates in high military office ?
What meaneth it that the coffers of the rich
are thrown open, and the earnings of the poor
eagerly proffered, and money has come to be
valued chiefly as an auxiliary to the successful
issue of our struggle, and the restoration of our
national prosperity ? I ask, what mean all
these things, if not that the nation is as strong
as she feels herself to be; that the fact that
her having determined that the Union *shull*
not be dissolved, conveys to us all the assur-
ance we need that, by God's blessing, it *will*
not be dissolved ? Especially, may I not say
this in view of the fact that the effort that is
now making to destroy our Government, is an
offence against the cherished memories of the

mighty dead; against the well-being of all coming generations; and, not least, against the righteousness and goodness of God? Yes, my friends, it is no presumption to believe that the Lord is on our side, and therefore our cause will certainly prosper.

But this conflict contemplates, in its issue, something more than the mere preservation of our Union,—the perpetuation of our institutions on their old basis. It looks towards progress. We have reason to believe that it is destined to originate a cure for some of our great national evils, as well as to otherwise greatly improve and exalt our national character. The greatest evil that, as a nation, we have had to encounter,—certainly the greatest, if measured by the amount of calamity which it has brought upon the country at large,—is Slavery. Scarcely a generation has passed away since the verdict of our Southern friends upon this institution was just what ours is now ;—that is, they saw in it an evil of appalling dimensions, from which the mass of them would gladly have been free, if a door of deliverance had been open ; but, since that time, the earth has been bringing forth a plant that has acted so strangely on their moral and mental vision, that that which they used to deprecate as a prolific source of evil, is now exalted into the rank of the highest positive blessings. None of us, even those who are most tolerant of the institution, believe that the light of the millenial day will dawn upon any husbands and wives, any parents and children, standing up like cattle to be examined by the traders in immortality, and then to hear the auctioneer's iron voice, revealing to them the fact that they are looking upon each others' faces for the last time. An institution which includes this among its provisions, all the generous instincts of our nature, to say nothing of the teachings of God's word, brand as a high offence against humanity. Nevertheless, this institution actually exists; aye, and exists under the shadow of the Constitution of the United States. Though the heart of a large part of the American people has bewailed this feature in our national condition, no one knew where to look for relief, so long as the Constitution should remain unchanged; and hence those convulsive spasms in favour of stealthy or forcible emancipation, into which a certain party at the North have been wrought, at the expense of showing themselves recreant to the laws of the land. But, if I mistake not, some beams of light begin now to penetrate this darkness. Not that you or I believe that we are sending armies to the South on any other mission than to maintain our Government, by putting down the rebellion that has assailed it; but there may be *incidental* results from this struggle, in which the death-warrant of the institution shall be written,—aye, and written by the very hands that were pledged to do their part in bearing it triumphantly onward to the end of time. It seems evident that the movement of our armies into the Southern country has already put new thoughts into the minds of many of the slaves; and it would not be strange if it had also awakened fresh aspirations for freedom— and who can say that these aspirations may not gradually ripen into purposes, and finally, (which may Heaven forbid,) into forcible and terrible acts? We hear of them also, in large numbers, actually coming within our lines; and I submit it to you whether the doctrine lately proclaimed by a distinguished military officer, and publicly sanctioned by the Secretary of War, and more recently by two other of our eminent citizens who have been marked for their conservatism,—that the slaves of rebel masters may be legitimately used for doing loyal work, is not a doctrine according to reason and justice. If it be said that the Constitution for which we are fighting makes no provision for our appropriating the labour of the slaves under any circumstances, I answer, the Constitution never contemplated the anomalous crisis that has overtaken us. War is a mighty, absolute potentate, that recognizes a law in its own necessities, and deals summarily with any code that interferes with that "higher law." What ultimate advantage to the cause of freedom, if any, shall result from this temporary interference with the workings of the institution, it must be left to Providence to determine. But the great fact, in the presence of which Slavery trembles most, is, that England, and the other European countries, are already looking to other parts of the world for a supply of the article to which the dreams of our Southern friends had given an almost omnipotent control; but the moment the sceptre departs from the hands of that flimsy king, the motive that has hitherto existed for the extension of Slavery, will give place to an equally powerful motive for its curtailment, if not its absolute extinction. We need not fear to leave the whole matter with Divine Providence—what we have to do is to prosecute the war for the end for which it has been inaugurated; and if, as an incidental consequence, Slavery should be shorn of a part or the whole of its strength, we shall none of us feel called upon to go into mourning.

But, whatever may be the effect of this war upon Slavery, we cannot doubt that it is to exert a mighty influence, in other ways, to elevate the character and destiny of our nation. Our long continued national prosperity had well-nigh dispossessed us of all that manly moral strength, that heroic love of country, which we had inherited from our fathers: it had made us idolaters of silver and gold; and, in worshipping at that ignoble shrine, all the finer, grander national qualities had become absolutely dwarfed. But the benefits of this fiery trial are already becoming apparent. Patriotism, which had become so weak and sickly as to be scarcely recognized, has renewed her strength, and is abroad, fulfilling her sublime mission wherever there are subjects to act upon,—no matter whether in the crowded city or the retired hamlet. The spirit of inglorious ease is dying out every where, and the spirit of noble self-sacrifice is coming in its place. Our young men are leaping for joy, to leave the blandishments of a pleasant home, that they may encounter the perils and sacrifices incident to the camp and battle field. Our old men are beginning to feel the beatings of young hearts again, and some of them are actually carrying muskets upon shoulders that have been bearing burdens for more than threescore years. Our matrons and maidens have found out that their country is something to *them;* and they are making it manifest that they are determined to be something to their *country.* By the discipline of his providence, God is teaching us lessons ot the highest wisdom,—especially to acknowledge our supreme allegiance to Him, and to identify all hopes of national prosperity with the enjoyment of his favour. Is not our country then, in this baptism of fire, undergoing a process of purification in every part of the intellectual and moral material that composes it ? Have we not a right to expect that our future will be brighter because of the darkness of the present; that out of this passing scene that seems so wild and chaotic, there will rise a new creation, that will make us, in a far higher sense than we have ever been before, the joy and praise of the whole earth ?

Yes, my friends, it is no vision,—it is a sublime reality, that we are contemplating. Do you not know how the literal furnace not only tries but purifies the precious metal that is cast into it ? Do you not know how the furnace of affliction separates the gold from the dross, in the case of the individual Christian,—throwing into a clear strong light those graces which had before seemed dubious, and lifting him into a far nobler specimen of the Divine workmanship than he had ever been before? Believe me, in these transforming processes is strikingly represented the glorious change that is now going forward amidst these deep shadows in which our land is embosomed. It is indeed a bloody storm that is raging. The watchman,

8

who is inquired of concerning the night, reports no signs of the morning yet. But things are all the time working, and the result will ere long be manifest. I wait a little, and the cloud begins to move, and presently I am gazing upon a clear bright sky. I see my country once more a unit;—all the wandering stars brought back into their spheres, and constituting a galaxy that even the angels love to gaze upon. I behold all the States bound together, not only in the bonds of a common sisterhood, but in a goodly ministration of blessing to each other and to the world. I see the great work of moral renovation advancing apace, until, by and by, a flood of millenial glory comes pouring in. And now begins the Jubilee, the great Thanksgiving Day, of the world. Oh, if my poor, bleeding country could, by the vision of faith, take in this grand prospect, sure I am that she would have no eye for the darkness of the present; no tongue but to make the mountains, and the vallies, and the forests, as well as the temples of the living God, echo to her grateful notes of praise !

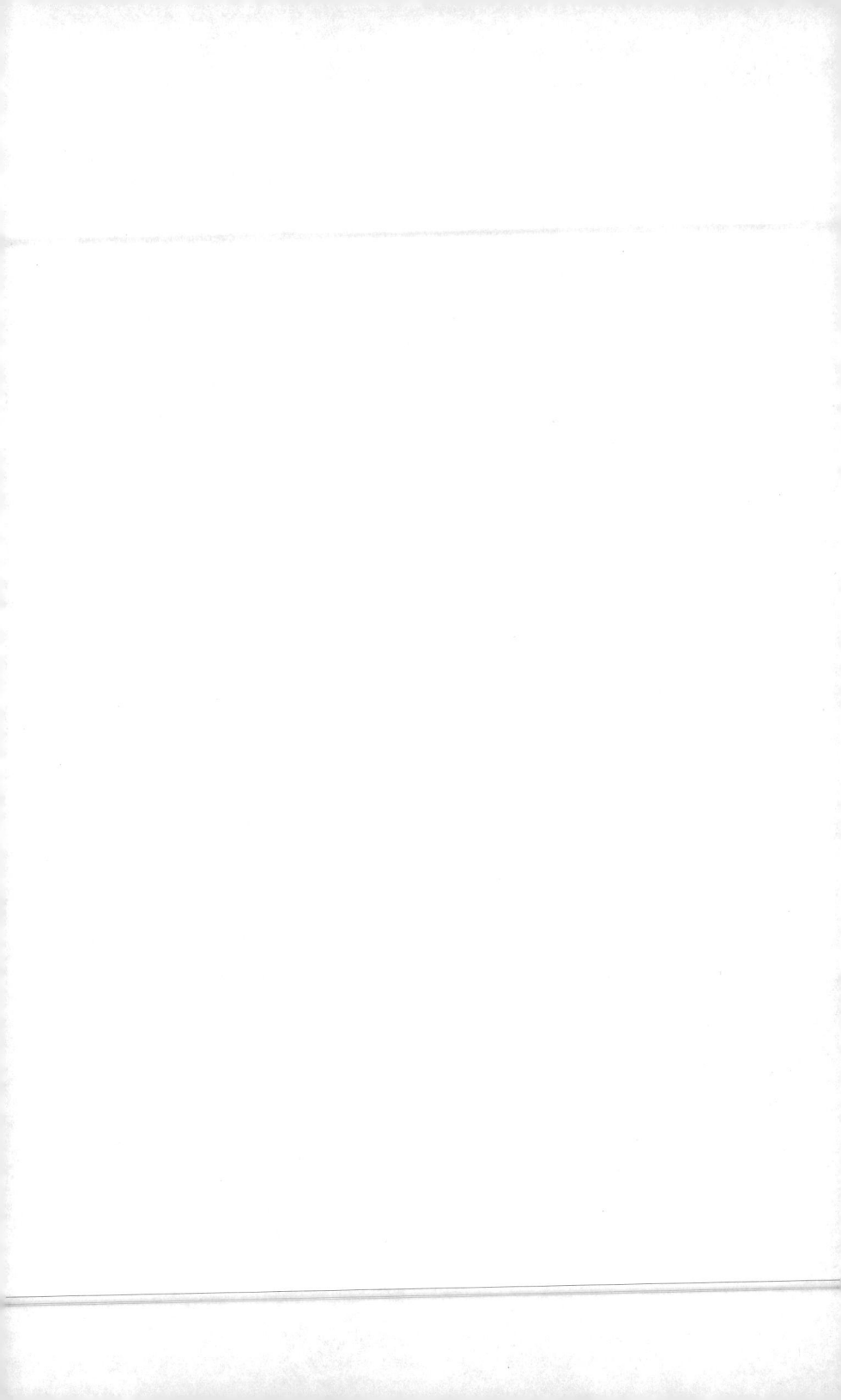

www.ingramcontent.com/pod-product-compliance
Lightning Source LLC
Chambersburg PA
CBHW031751090426
42739CB00008B/971